LIVE INSPIRED TO EMPOWER, INSPIRE
AND BE TRULY RELECTIVE

DR. MOTIVATE

101 DAYS

OF INSPIRATION

Copyright © 2019 Donald Ray Brown, Jr. Ph.D.

All rights reserved. No part of this publication may be reproduced, distributed, or transmitted in any form or by any means, including photocopying, recording, or other electronic or mechanical methods, without the prior written permission of the publisher, except in the case of brief quotations embodied in critical reviews and certain other noncommercial uses permitted by copyright law.

ISBN-13: 978-1-970079-39-5

Published and Cover Design by:
Opportune Independent Publishing Co.
113 N. Live Oak Street
Houston, TX 77003
(832) 263-1700
www.opportunepublishing.com

Let's Engage

Let us know if we can help you with your next Keynote, Motivational Speaking Engagement, Corporate Leadership Training, Professional Development, Athletic Seminars or Customized Training Solutions.

Contact us by Email: brownandassociates1@yahoo.com or by visiting our website: www.drmotivate.org

As a cutting-edge educator, aspiring best-selling author, and a dynamic speaker, Dr. Motivate, is cultivating an extensive following amongst some of the most highly respected and influential leaders around the world. Reaching thousands of people yearly through speaking engagements alone, he is committed to giving children, students and adults hope; while providing those he has the opportunity to impact with the finest resources and training for personal and professional growth.

Let's stay connected as you read! I have four challenges for you! Are you ready? Okay here goes:

Challenge 1: On social media hashtag your favorite Dr. Motivate quotes using #DrMotivate101

Challenge 2: Take a picture of yourself reading 101 Days of Inspiration and use the hashtag #DrMotivate101Pic

Challenge 3: Record a video of how you have used 101 Days of Inspiration to help yourself and others. Use the hashtag #DrMotivate101Power

Challenge 4: Ask Dr. Motivate to consider using a personal quote you created in one of his future publications by using the hashtag #DrMotivate101PleaseUseMyQuote

(By completing any of the four challenges, you are giving consent for Dr. Motivate and affiliates to consider using what you created through the challenge in future projects).

—Dr. Motivate

www.drmotivate.org

- www.youtube.com/channel/UCF211kZriU-J6I0-zhQ6HVWw
- @DrMotivate1
- @DrMotivate
- @DrMotivate1
- DrMotivate
- www.linkedin.com/in/donald-brown-73984227

Day 1

Do what you don't want to do! So, you can do what you want to do! Tunechi.

- Dr. Motivate

(Quote from Lil'Wayne)

Day 2

Evaluate your inner circle your future and life depend on it! You've got to run after your destiny and remain committed.

– Dr. Motivate

Day 3

Don't skip steps in the process. Through the struggle will come something greater!

- Dr. Motivate

Day 4

Your Dreams Must Wake You Up!

- Dr. Motivate

Day 5

Don't be distracted. Keep chopping wood or carry water. You can't do both at the same time!

- Dr. Motivate

Day 6

Glorious victories don't just happen without contending with unbearable adversity!

– Dr. Motivate

Day 7

Your actions prove who you are; words just prove who you want to be.

– Dr. Motivate

Day 8

Remember your FOCUS now... determines your REALITY later.

– Dr. Motivate

Day 9

Many start STRONG...few FINISH...which one, are YOU?

- Dr. Motivate

Day 10

Let nothing stop your grind! It might take 12 years to get to that one year that will change your life!

– Dr. Motivate

Day 11

Passion paves a pathway for your success!

- Dr. Motivate

Day 12

Repeated success or failure can be measured by one's insanity!

– Dr. Motivate

Day 13

Don't let no negative thought, negative person or negative circumstance keep you from running after your goals with insanity! Your best is near, and your better will be best!

– Dr. Motivate

Day 14

You are what you do, not what you say you will do!

– Dr. Motivate

Day 15

Do what you – LOVE – what you do!

– Dr. Motivate

101 DAYS

Challenge 1:

On social media hashtag your favorite Dr. Motivate quotes using #DrMotivate101

Day 16

The average minded will call you insane, brilliant people will call you for guidance!

− Dr. Motivate

Day 17

Focus on the Cause & Utilize your Strength!

– Dr. Motivate

Day 18

When you get punched in the mouth, it's your preparation & follow through that you fall back on!

- Dr. Motivate

Day 19

Today is the day; I own my future's future. I will not stop, no matter how difficult it is.

– Dr. Motivate

Day 20

Let your passion fuel your instinctive drive to win!

- Dr. Motivate

Day 21

I won't stop until what needs to be done is FINISHED!

- Dr. Motivate

Day 22

You won't do big things if you get distracted by small things. Stay FOCUSED!

- Dr. Motivate

Day 23

Your actions will always beat your intentions, Follow-Through!

– Dr. Motivate

Day 24

The secret to winning is finishing what you start, even when you don't feel like it.

– Dr. Motivate

Day 25

Champions FOCUS on what they want, not what they don't have.

– Dr. Motivate

Day 26

Follow-Through defeats Procrastination. Period!

- Dr. Motivate

Day 27

Nothing else matters when you FINISH what you START!

- Dr. Motivate

Day 28

Find your fire, live your PASSION!

– Dr. Motivate

Day 29

Practice the things others don't want to do, over and over again. You will win!

– Dr. Motivate

Day 30

Focus on the right things, not the things that scream the loudest!

– Dr. Motivate

101 DAYS

Day 31

Your Follow-Through must be so strong; it will chop wood without an ax!

- Dr. Motivate

Day 32

FINISH! Stop Talking.

– Dr. Motivate

Day 33

Passion Produces Purpose! Now soar above, things that don't matter.

- Dr. Motivate

Day 34

Insanity gives you the right, to lose your mind for your Dream!

– Dr. Motivate

Day 35

Distractions keep you on Plan C which distracts from Plan A. Stay Focused!

- Dr. Motivate

Day 36

When your actions become muscle memory, your follow-through will scare your enemies.

– Dr. Motivate

Day 37

When you are a finisher, opportunities will come to find you.

- Dr. Motivate

Day 38

Allow your energy to glow, and the help you need will find you.

– Dr. Motivate

Day 39

Is that what they believe? Well, maybe you should quit because my soul just screamed: "I Ain't Gonna LOSE"!

– Dr. Motivate

Challenge 2:

Take a picture of yourself reading 101 Days of Inspiration and use the hashtag #DrMotivate101Pic

Day 40

When you lack FOCUS, you will fail to make your goals a priority. Stay FOCUSED!

- Dr. Motivate

Day 41

When you are a finisher, you don't fight to the finish. You fight through the process of becoming the best that any eye has ever seen.

– Dr. Motivate

Day 42

When dreams are fueled by passion, the vision stays alive, and a lot happens.

- Dr. Motivate

Day 43

Sometimes you must be willing to give uphanging out, to live your dreams! You are the one, now make it happen!

- Dr. Motivate

Day 44

Focus takes effort, if an effort to focus lacks, you will live a leprechaun's reality unfulfilled.

- Dr. Motivate

Day 45

Finishers are "Game Changers"! Do you have what it takes to finish?

- Dr. Motivate

Day 46

Your passion will attract things to you, that you have only imagined in your dreams!

– Dr. Motivate

Day 47

It's crazy until your actions and faith push you to accomplish what others won't even try. Believe that you can, then do it!

– Dr. Motivate

Day 48

When things are tough FOCUS will clarify your picture, as negatives always develop a better picture.

— Dr. Motivate

Day 49

Follow-Through determines the difference. "Through the struggle will come something greater!"

- Dr. Motivate

Day 50

Finishers don't stop. They don't quit. They don't abort the dream. They win with actions, determination, discipline, faith, commitment and running in possibilities.

- Dr. Motivate

Day 51

Passion breathes life into your dreams. Let the world discover, what only you have seen. You are the dream!

- Dr. Motivate

Day 52

Live your dreams! You are the one, now make it happen!

– Dr. Motivate

Day 53

When breakthrough is near, the enemy will use what worked in the past to shift your focus. Don't fall for it. Stay focused anyway.

– Dr. Motivate

Day 54

Design the life you want to live, by following through on the things you need to live. You can do it.

- Dr. Motivate

Day 55

I'm a finisher; I don't care about what you think, say or do. I care about finishing the right way, always, every day.

– Dr. Motivate

Day 56

When you ignite everything, you touch with passion & confidence, you will be remembered. Now Let's Go Get It!

− Dr. Motivate

Day 57

Run after your dreams like your clothes are on fire! Others will come to assist you in fulfilling your heart's desire.

- Dr. Motivate

Day 58

People will wonder, how do they do that? When you focus and intentionally move pass problems that weren't meant for you. The secret is Don't Lose Your FOCUS!

– Dr. Motivate

Day 59

Do you want to dominate in life? Do you want others to trust at your word? If you said YES, then it's simple...all you have to do is Follow-Through. Step into your greatness.

- Dr. Motivate

Day 60

So, what do they think about your goal? People think that it's hard. It's not. It's just different. Be different. Finish what you started.

– Dr. Motivate

Day 61

If you are not eating with me, you are likely part of the meal!

– Dr. Motivate

Day 62

You will not rise to the expectation; you will rise to your level of training. Train hard!

– Dr. Motivate

Day 63

Don't let anything steal your passion. Learn to let it go.

- Dr. Motivate

Day 64

When your dream is upstream, then go upstream to get it. Remember, it's your dream.

– Dr. Motivate

Day 65

Evaluate your inner circle; they should always want you to win. Your circle should be your biggest cheerleader when you face hard times. If this is not happening, find a new circle.

– Dr. Motivate

Day 66

To be the scholar of what you do, it requires FOCUS. Turn the noise off on purpose.

- Dr. Motivate

Day 67

When you get tired, still follow-through. Your future depends on it.

- Dr. Motivate

Day 68

Don't quit. FINISH. Don't procrastinate. FINISH. Don't hope. FINISH. Don't wait for someone else. FINISH. Do what's hard to do. Always FINISH.

- Dr. Motivate

Day 69

How do I find my passion?
You see it by recognizing and
owning the things in life that
make your heart vibrate with joy.

– Dr. Motivate

Challenge 3:

Record a video of how you have used 101 Days of Inspiration to help yourself and others. Use the hashtag #DrMotivate101Power

Day 70

When you dream about it throughout the day, and you find yourself staying up at night, you are now living in the realm of passion. I challenge you to take action now by writing out steps that bring your passion to life.

– Dr. Motivate

Day 71

People will doubt you. Dream it anyway. They'll say you are unrealistic. Visualize it happening anyway. They'll say no way. Take action anyway and smile all day.

- Dr. Motivate

Day 72

Come from amongst them. Don't be afraid. Be different. It's time for the world to see and know who you are.

- Dr. Motivate

Day 73

When you are in an uncomfortable place, it is your FOCUS that will pull you out. Don't pay attention to the noise. Just focus.

- Dr. Motivate

Day 74

Shhhhh. Here's the secret to competitive advantage. FOLLOW-THROUGH!

- Dr. Motivate

Day 75

Uncommonly. Become. Common.

- Dr. Motivate

Day 76

It's decision time. Look in the mirror and ask, "Am I going to or Am I not going to?" It's just that simple. Make a decision. Finishing requires EFFORT!

- Dr. Motivate

Day 77

Have you discovered your passion? Passion can reboot the positive energy needed, to move you past moments of exhaustion. Know this, and you will overcome.

- Dr. Motivate

Day 78

You cannot become, what you cannot see.

– Dr. Motivate

Day 79

Your pinky toe is infected. It will damage the rest of your body. You must be willing to cut the pinky toe off. When will you make the cuts? Greatness requires INSANE sacrifice.

- Dr. Motivate

Day 80

Continue to focus. Things are changing for you. Remember this is a marathon, not a sprint. Keep your focus.

- Dr. Motivate

Day 81

When you only do what's easy, you'll never accomplish what's hard.

– Dr. Motivate

Day 82

Remember me? I came to you in a dream. Yes, you started, but you left me there. I'm now a mystery when I should be a part of his-story. FOLLOW-THROUGH!

- Dr. Motivate

Day 83

Finishing has everything to do with not letting yourself and others depending on you down. When things get tough. FINISH anyway.

– Dr. Motivate

Day 84

When it comes to making a life change. Winning is a decision. Losing is a choice.

— Dr. Motivate

Day 85

When your passion fuels your most intimate thoughts. You will be seen before you can be seen. Don't be surprised. Just keep working.

- Dr. Motivate

Day 86

When you say you want to be the best, do you really mean it? What things do you do before and after your 9-5? Stop talking & do.

- Dr. Motivate

Day 87

Do I hear you saying, "I want to accomplish more?" I challenge you to put 100% focus into completing one task, before adding another task. Now FOCUS.

- Dr. Motivate

Day 88

Don't worry, if you keep following-through and exerting full effort. The reward will come. They are still going to hate, Follow-Through anyway.

- Dr. Motivate

Day 89

Finish so hard; it makes your enemies question their existence.

– Dr. Motivate

Day 90

"PASSION"- They don't understand why you keep going. They are not supposed to. Only you. Work like tomorrow doesn't exist. Keep knocking your goals off their wish list.

- Dr. Motivate

101 DAYS

Day 91

"INSANITY"- You against Me? Me against You? I'm about to beat your P.ersonal B.est R.ecord! Are you serious! Try Me! Look in the mirror; I'm your competition.

- Dr. Motivate

Day 92

Focus - Three distractions. Three things are unnoticed. Three opportunities. Three things capitalized on. Choose what you give your FOCUS.

- Dr. Motivate

Day 93

Follow-Through- I will check on you. I will watch you. I will come after you. Until you are done and done is finished.

- Dr. Motivate

Day 94

FINISH – When you challenge me, the competition is 100 % OVER. I hate losing more than I enjoy winning. While you were sleep, I defeated you by doing another thousand reps.

– Dr. Motivate

Day 95

When your passion speaks louder than your words, "Actions" birth results, despite the struggle.

– Dr. Motivate

Challenge 4:

Ask Dr. Motivate to consider using a personal quote you created in one of his future publications by using the hashtag #DrMotivate101PleaseUseMyQuote

Day 96

Stay in love with the process, even when it seems improbable. Remember people will judge you, it's just part of the process.

- Dr. Motivate

Day 97

When you can see through the storm, the rain won't bother you. Don't lose your FOCUS. You are the Storm. So let it rain!

- Dr. Motivate

Day 98

Master vs. Wannabe: The Master has tried, failed, gotten back up, tried again, then succeeded and taught someone else how. Wannabe has no follow-through. Period.

– Dr. Motivate

Day 99

Truth – The only place "Win" comes before "Work" is in the dictionary.

– Dr. Motivate

Day 100

Experience – The setback will not define you; it's how you respond that will. So, endure the challenge one second longer than defeat.

– Dr. Motivate

Day 101

Passion – My tank is on E., but it just won't turn off, until I win!

– Dr. Motivate

www.ingramcontent.com/pod-product-compliance
Lightning Source LLC
Chambersburg PA
CBHW071902070526
44583CB00016B/1799